Lent and the Pilgrim

Lent and the Pilgrim

15 Bible Studies for Lent and Easter

Reverend Rosalie Weller

Pink and Purple

Scripture quotations taken from The Holy Bible, New International Version ®NIV®
Copyright© 1973197819842011 by Biblica,Inc.TM used by permission.

ISBN-9798703239452

Cover design by www.samwellerillustrations.com
Cover photo by Rosalie Weller

Dedicated to Daisy Weller.
She is a seeker of the truth and the Lord
and a worthy example of a Christian pilgrim

ENDORSEMENTS

"The writer's exposition of the Holy Week in Lent covers crucial themes and concepts of Christianity. Rosalie Weller gives scriptural examples that convincingly back up facts on these concepts. She often uses unique and insightful examples as well as providing questions which help to develop one's relationship with God. A read which certainly blesses the reader. A highly recommended book.
(Olusola Sophia Anyanwa, Author)

"Here is a study guide that provides all that you need to journey through scripture from the start of Lent through to Easter week. Clear teaching on core Christian principles and thought-provoking questions will provide plenty of discussion points making it ideal for small groups.
(Sharon Hazel, blogger)

Table of Contents

Introduction

Lent is a special time of year for Christians, so come on a spiritual journey with me. As we reflect on Jesus' journey to his death and begin a detailed examination of Holy Week, we will draw nearer to Jesus. For many, especially children, Easter is about chocolate eggs. Does that matter? The egg, which resembles a stone, can prompt a conversation about the stone in front of Jesus' tomb. Just as God indulges us, as children, let the children enjoy the chocolate. What better way to celebrate than by eating chocolate! But before we get there, several less pleasant topics must be discussed.

Traditionally Lent focuses on the sacrifice Jesus made for us, beginning with his temptation in the desert. I have included this for study but have chosen some additional topics which I believe are also important. For the disciples, Holy Week was about dread and fear for their own lives. It was about disappointment and sadness. We study the horrific events of the week, but unlike them, we know the ending is resurrection. So, we can study in the knowledge of the coming celebration. Put aside your traditional preconceptions and join me on this year's journey. Begin afresh and embrace both sorrow and joy with Jesus and his disciples. Each study has a title which **summarises where the study is in the context of the whole.** On the next line, is one word which you should apply personally to yourself as you read the comments and go on to the questions.

Peter describes Christians as pilgrims (I Peter 2: 11-12). We must hold on lightly to the things of this world if we want to progress in our spiritual lives. Lent is a special time when we have the opportunity to do this.

This study is not intended just to improve your head knowledge, although I hope it does. It is my aim to challenge your heart and spiritual life. Try to spend some time before you start **each** study, alone in prayer. It may be just five minutes but do it. Come out of the busy world and focus on God.

Psalm 103:1
Praise the Lord, O my soul;
All my inmost being, praise His holy name.

BIBLE STUDY 1 - Ash Wednesday

REPENTANCE

Read: Psalm 51

Ash Wednesday is an important date in the Church of England and Catholic liturgical calendar. It is not always celebrated in other Protestant denominations, especially not in Free churches. Do not worry if your group do not mark the day off as special. It is a matter of tradition and custom.

Shrove Tuesday has been absorbed by our common culture. Many households celebrate by eating pancakes even if they don't know the religious significance behind the day. Some villages, for example Olney in Northants, celebrate with an annual pancake race. Pancake day is a celebration which occurs before the sacrifices to be made during Lent.

The title of this psalm explains the context of it. David wrote it when he was confronted by Nathan the prophet about his adultery with Bathsheba. Nathan's story can be found in 2 Samuel chapter 12. As Nathan recounts the story of the two lambs, it does not occur to David that he is the perpetrator of an evil deed. In 12:7 David is left in no doubt. Isn't it so like us, human beings? We become enraged when we hear about someone else's sin but we are often guilty too. Think about the steps of repentance we find in Psalm 51.

Firstly, David acknowledges his need for cleansing. Verses 1 and 2 ask for cleansing. It is an admission of guilt. In verse 3 he is aware of his sin. He realises that it is a greater sin to sin against God than against people. Yes, he has wronged Uriah but he has also broken several commandments, i.e., adultery and murder.

David pleads with God for pardon verses 7-9. He acknowledges the punishment he deserves. In verses 11-12 David realises that his sin has disrupted his relationship with God and the precariousness of his soul.

In verses 13-17 David is more positive and hopeful, realising God can be merciful. He promises to help and teach others. Finally in verses 18-19 David widens his horizons to the city of Zion and its sacrificial system. He promises God he will become a help instead of a hindrance.

BIBLE STUDY 1 – Questions

TESTING THE FACTS

1. What sin did David commit? 2 Samuel 12

2. What punishment did God give David?

GIVING YOUR VIEW

1. Did you attend an Ash Wednesday service? If you did, describe the service and give your view of the experience. Share with the group.

2. What do you understand by the word, 'repentance'?

3. Do you think David received an adequate and appropriate punishment? Share your view with the group.

For you alone

Take this opportunity to review your life using psalm 51:

    v. 1-2 acknowledge your need for cleansing,

    v. 3-6 what sin/s have you committed against

    God? Use the 10 commandments as a

reference point.

BIBLE STUDY 2 – First Sunday of Lent

FASTING

Read Matthew 6: 16-21

The time of Lent is particularly associated with fasting. In the modern age when we think about fasting, we mean that we intend to give up something we enjoy. In the Protestant tradition though, fasting means going without water and food, for a prolonged period of time. The absence of nourishment to the body heightens spiritual awareness. It brings you closer to God.

Today, however, some people consider giving up mobile phones or technology as a form of fasting. The concept has moved away from the hunger pains and desire to satisfy hunger, to going without something you enjoy. We have moved away from submission to God to self-denial. Is it really the same thing? Eating is a basic necessity for the body. Technology is not.

In the passage, by his use of the preposition "when", Jesus implies that fasting is something in which a disciple will regularly participate. Jesus recommends how this should be done. If a pilgrim is serious about wanting to worship God, it will be a private meeting not a public display. The Pharisees wanted people to see how devout they were so their sombre faces reminded people they were fasting.

Fasting is an activity for a specific time and place. Some Christians reserve it as a special time at Lent, as a prerequisite for the approaching Easter celebration. John Wesley insisted that Christian ministers serving in the Methodist denomination fast for two days a week, all year round. That meant no food from sundown one day to 3pm the next day. Water was allowed. This is a practice almost unheard of within ministerial circuits today. Of course, fasting is a regular practice in the month of Ramadan for Muslims.

BIBLE STUDY 2 – Questions

TESTING THE FACTS

1.What is the occasion of these comments by Jesus about fasting?

2.What are the conditions of fasting according to Jesus?

GIVING YOUR VIEW

1.What is your concept of fasting? Is the denial of enjoyment the same thing as denial of food and water? Share your views with the group.

2.When should your fasting be disclosed to another person? Is it ok when it is to encourage another believer?

3.Do you think that people in Christian ministry or Christian leadership roles should fast regularly as John Wesley recommended? Give reasons and share your views with the group.

4.Read Jesus' comments where his disciples are compared with those of John the Baptist's and the Pharisees (Matthew 9:14-17). What does Jesus say about fasting on this occasion? How does this affect us today?

FURTHER RESEARCH
1. Compare Christian fasting with Muslim fasting.

PRAYER
Heavenly Father
Help us, Lord, to approach Lent with a sincere heart. May each one of us grow in our faith through this study. We pray for those who do not know you. Help us, Lord, to be good examples of Christians.

In the name of our Lord Jesus Christ and in the power of the Holy Spirit.
AMEN

Testimony

As many of you will know, I went to South Africa in 1982 to accompany my husband who joined the South African Navy. We were a blended family. Three of our children were biologically my husband's, one was biologically mine and we had another child in September of that year. It was a new start for us in a new country. For many years God blessed us, not materially, we scrimped quite a lot, but as a family. We grew in love and fellowship amongst ourselves and with the Christian community. Of course, it required a lot of effort on everyone's part. All seven of us had our interests and funny ways!

Our previous spouses stayed in touch with the children occasionally. Then after a long time one of my husband's ex-spouse's family members decided that a visit was desirable. The children were still very young and changing countries, making new friends and fitting in with each other had been a big challenge for all of them. So, I became worried. How would such a visit affect the children? I began to pray about it. Then I decided because of the conflicting emotions within me, I should fast as well. What did the Lord want for our family and our children? It is good for children to stay in touch with their natural parents but they also need to bond with their new family members. I wasn't sure this was a good time for a visit and all the emotional upheaval that would bring.

I had taken part in occasional fasting before and always found it beneficial. So, I began to fast. I drank only herbal tea and no food for the first three days, then just eating a light evening meal. All the time, I prayed, what O Lord do you want for this family? The day of the visit drew nearer. Still God did not seem to answer. Then on the day of the visit we heard the couple could not get on the plane to South Africa as the male had spontaneous bleeding from various orifices in the body. He was admitted to hospital and told to rest. The doctors could find no reason for his condition and the holiday was cancelled. I did not ask the Lord to make the couple ill. I just asked that God would intervene in His own way so that my children would not be hurt. I offer no explanation for these events. I just recall them as they happened. Draw your own conclusions

.

BIBLE STUDY 3 - Second Sunday of Lent

TEMPTATION

Read Matthew 4: 1-11 - The Temptations of Jesus

The bible instructs us that suffering accompanies temptation. We wrestle with the desire to do good and the temptation to do bad. Jesus experienced this so that he understands what we go through when we are tempted in every way. So, as we consider the temptations, we can be reassured that Jesus knows our struggles (Hebrews 2:18).

Beneath temptation is the desire to do wrong which we must understand if we are to overcome temptation. We each have a different weakness but all of them are encompassed in these temptations. Often a person struggles with the same weakness time and time again. Reflect on Genesis 4:7 ("If you do what is right, will you not be accepted? But if you do not do what is right, sin is crouching at your door. It desires to have you, but you must master it.") to come to grips with this idea.

The temptations are divided into three kinds. If we can recognise them as temptations, we can guard against them and overcome them through the power of the Holy Spirit.

1. The devil tempts Jesus to satisfy his hunger by turning the stones into bread to eat. When you are hungry it is indeed tempting to grab the first thing that comes to hand, as many dieters will tell you. The body does need food but this need can be abused, as we see in people suffering either from anorexia or obesity. All the bodily functions can be abused.

2. Jesus challenges this by pointing out that the Word of God is more important than satisfying hunger, under certain circumstances. Denial of food directly links to this first temptation. That is why fasting is such a powerful discipline. Hence, I argue in Bible Study 2 whether giving up technology is the same as giving up food and drink. Jesus seems to be pointing out that we can control our bodily functions and must do so.

3. The second temptation presents the situation of a desperate plea for God's rescue in the face of reckless human activity. Jesus knows he has been sent by God. Yes, God may well save him from self-destruction but he is not at liberty to test God in that way. Yes, Daniel was saved from the jaws of a lion and Paul was not harmed by a poisonous snake but they did not recklessly assume God would protect their bodily safety. They were forced into those circumstances. They did not choose them.

Jesus answers, "Do not test God". God will help us as He wills. But if we deliberately put ourselves in danger, we may have to face the consequences without His rescue. In modern terms, do not coerce and manipulate God to get your own way. It is a form of arrogance. It is a 'party trick' mentality.

There is a link of this temptation with our human condition which we must accept. Human beings are mortal; they don't live for ever. The body is subject to destruction. Many people find this hard to accept, even though they know it intellectually.

4. Thirdly, the devil tempts Jesus by offering wealth, success and worldly power in exchange for worship. Jesus points out that we are instructed to worship only God. The subtlety of the temptation is that as humans we are so easily beguiled by money and power. This temptation is particularly noticeable in Western society which is so materialistic. We can be lulled into a search for riches and power without being conscious of it.

PRAYER
Almighty God
We need your help to be aware of temptation, especially that which arises from our human condition. Help us in our weakness. Lord Jesus. Thank you that you have gone before us and there is nothing about temptation which you do not understand. Holy Spirit, convict us of our sin and cleanse us.
AMEN

BIBLE STUDY 3 – Questions

TESTING THE FACTS

1. Name the three temptations which Jesus underwent?

2. Write out the scripture verses which Jesus gave to combat these temptations.

GIVING YOUR VIEW

1. Examine yourself in relation to the temptations (Bodily functions, mortality or riches and power). Where is your weakness? Complete this task yourself over the next few days.

2. Give some modern-day examples of the three temptations. Share your ideas with the group.

3. Do you think it is useful to recite scripture in the face of temptation?

4. Do you memorise scripture verses? Share with the group. Over the Lent period resolve to learn some scripture verses, perhaps from the Psalms.

5. The second temptation is difficult to understand. Think of a modern-day example.

6. Thinking of the third temptation, what does it mean to worship something or someone? Discuss in the group.

RESEARCH
James 1: 2-18: No one should say, "God is tempting me". Research what the bible says about testing and temptation. Is there a difference?

Psalm 6; 1-2
O Lord, do not rebuke me in your anger
Or discipline me in your wrath
Be merciful to me, Lord,
For I am faint;
O Lord, heal me, for my bones are in agony.

BIBLE STUDY 4 - Third Sunday in Lent

EVIL
Read Luke 11: 14-28 Jesus and Beelzebub

In this passage there is a clear dichotomy between the two forces - good and evil. The question has to be considered, if God created the world, did He create evil? This is a question which has been considered by many scholars from Augustine to C. S. Lewis.

We can find many examples of substances which when used in small quantities can be helpful to humans but when administered in larger doses would prove fatal. For example, morphine in controlled doses can be used for pain relief but in large doses will kill you. In this way we can realise that God must have created things which can be used for evil. It is not God who commits the evil but that humans have the potential for evil inside them. Consider the story of Cain and Abel. Cain had the potential for evil inside of him and he made the decision to act in an evil way and murder his brother.

We may also not understand when a tsunami or earthquake kills people or a volcano erupts. But the earth has a physical structure which is continually developing and reacting. Scientists study and can predict natural phenomena before they occur and can warn people but they cannot stop the natural event from happening.

Also, in this passage we read about the phenomena of evil spirits. In the western world we are loathe to believe in such happenings. I have been in Africa and witnessed first hand oppression by evil spirits just once in a journey of 40 years as a Christian. It does happen today but we are sceptical and rightly so. Spiritual possession should not be tackled unless you are experienced with such matters. The Church of England has priests specifically trained to deal with these things, as do other denominations.

In this passage Jesus does explain, that just as supernatural healing relies on God's power, so there are powers which have evil effects. This evil spirit is referred to as a mute spirit and Jesus is accused of gaining power to deal with it from the devil. But the logic of Jesus' explanation is undeniable. Any power divided against itself will fall. If Jesus was from Satan, he would not have healed the man but would have left the evil spirit in him. Therefore, Jesus cannot be from the devil.

Another lesson is that when a power (spirit) is taken out, it leaves a vacuum and all sorts of evil can take up that space. Hence, we must be filled with the Holy Spirit (Ephesians 5:18). We need to come before the Lord daily.

Verse 27 is curious, as the woman blesses Jesus' mother. You would think, that would be a wonderful thing to say. But Jesus rebukes her and commends only those who hear the word of God and obey.

In this third week of Lent, we are made aware of the presence of evil and spiritual forces. It is not a subject to dwell on but it is important to know what the bible says about it.

PRAYER

Heavenly Father
This week we ask you to help us discern the
spiritual forces present in the world and to fill us
with the Holy Spirit, so we may be guided by you
in everything we do. Lead us not into temptation
but deliver us from evil.
We ask this in the name of Jesus, our Lord and
Saviour.
AMEN

BIBLE STUDY 4 – Questions

TESTING THE FACTS

1.What does Jesus say causes the man's dumbness?

2.What defence does Jesus give when accused of working for the devil (Beelzebub)?

3.When does this event take place? (What is the context?)

GIVING YOUR VIEW

1. Do you believe there are evil spirits? Give examples and share with the group.

2. Could this man be described in modern day terms as suffering from 'selective mutism' or a related physical or mental illness? Discuss.

3. There sometimes seems to be a resemblance between the symptoms of a person suffering

from mental illness and people having evil spirits. Share your ideas in the group.

RESEARCH

Read Ephesians 6: 10-12

"For our struggle is not against flesh and blood, but against the rulers, against the authorities, against the powers of this dark world and against the spiritual forces of evil in the heavenly realms." Examine what this means.

BIBLE STUDY 5 - Fourth Week of Lent

SACRIFICE

Read at least one of the following:
Luke 3: 1-20 - Repent
Matthew 11: 1-19 Are you the Christ?
Matthew 14: 1-13 The Platter

It may seem strange to study John the Baptist for a Lent series but he epitomises a self-sacrificing individual, who had a ministry specialising in repentance. John tells the people to turn away from their sin and turn towards God. In this study there are many strands to consider. What does Lent mean in terms of servanthood and self-denial? What does sacrifice mean? Jesus says if we want to be disciples, we must deny ourselves, take up our cross and then follow Him (Luke 9:23). John the Baptist makes the ultimate sacrifice in that he gives up his life in pursuit of the truth. He also sacrifices his ministry so Jesus can supersede him.

The readings follow the ministry of John and each part of that ministry is considered as you study the questions. Reading 1 is John's initial ministry and his lifestyle. Reading 2 outlines when he was in prison and sent his disciples to Jesus to confirm that Jesus was indeed the Messiah. Jesus' answer echoes the passage in Isaiah 61: 1, which would have been known to both of them. Reading 3 outlines the process of his untimely death.

Herodias was married to a successful politician Herod Philip. When his brother comes to stay there is a fatal attraction. Herod Antipas persuades Herodias to leave her husband and live with him. It was not only a question of adultery. Under Jewish law it was also forbidden to marry one's brother's wife while the brother was still living. John the Baptist knew that this couple's actions were wrong. He paid with his life for that confrontation.

Also, we reflect on the different styles of ministry as modelled by John the Baptist and Jesus. We can be encouraged in that as we realise there is not only one style of ministry. Jesus calls each one of us to walk in our own individual paths within a community.

Underlying this study is John the Baptist's message of repentance - one which we must also heed. Repentance means to change one's mind. We must change our worldly minds and start to think like God does.

PRAYER

Almighty God
We come to you in the name of Jesus Christ and in full submission. Help us understand what sacrifice means and how we can deny ourselves to make some sacrifice. Help us to put ourselves aside and concentrate on you.

AMEN

BIBLE STUDY 5 – Questions

TESTING THE FACTS

1. Name three qualities of John the Baptist's lifestyle. (Matthew 3: 1-12)

2. What question did John's disciples ask Jesus?

3. What did Salome ask for after she had danced for Herod Antipas?

GIVING YOUR VIEW

1. Jesus challenges John to weigh up the evidence to assess whether he is the promised Messiah. What detailed evidence would you give John?

2. Do you identify more with the ministry of John the Baptist, pious and dedicated or with Jesus unconventional and relaxed? Give reasons for your answer and share with the group.

3. John the Baptist was not afraid to denounce Herodias' adultery even though it cost him his life. How would you have reacted in a similar situation? Share with the group.

4. Affairs and divorce are commonplace in our society today. How do you respond?

5. John the Baptist's message was one of repentance and baptism. Compare the values of the world with the values of God, in the group. On an individual basis, examine how far your values fall short of God's.

Psalm 51:10
Create in me a pure heart, O God,
And renew a steadfast spirit within me.
Do not cast me from your presence
Or take your Holy Spirit from me.
Restore to me the joy of your salvation
And grant me a willing spirit to sustain me.

BIBLE STUDY 6 - Palm Sunday

DOUBLE-MINDEDNESS

Read Luke 19: 28-44 The Triumphal Entry

Within the context of the entry into Jerusalem, we follow Jesus through Jericho where He interacts with Zaccheus and teaches the people through a parable. He stops at Bethpage and Bethany, and instructs two disciples to get a colt. In John's account of this story, it is recorded that the day before his entry into Jerusalem, Jesus goes to the house of Lazarus, Martha and Mary, where Mary anoints Jesus with perfume. (John 12: 12-15). We look at this part of the story in detail in study 8.

Jesus carefully choreographs his entry into Jerusalem by riding on a colt. The Jewish people were well versed in their scriptures and traditions. The gesture does not go unnoticed.

Jesus is a celebrity as he enters Jerusalem. Everyone has heard about the miracles he has performed. They are praising God because of them. Surely this is an authentic response to Jesus. The Pharisees want to silence the people but as Jesus points out in verse 40, "the stones would cry out", if the people were silent. God himself has been silent for four hundred years. Now He speaks by sending His Son. But it is less than a week later when the crowds are baying for Jesus' blood.

When we read this particular story, we can consider the importance of places. The sight of this great city of David moves Jesus to tears. It is the centre of Judaism. Jesus recognises its past glories and its shortcomings. Also, to consider, is the fickleness of people which is apparent in the wider context of this story. Although some commentators say it is not the same crowd who rejoice and then later condemn. I likewise think the people who praise Jesus on his entry are not the same as the people who condemn him. Those who praised Him had seen his miracles. That is not an easy sight to forget.

Double-mindedness can happen if you are easily influenced. One day you will want to go one way and the next day, the other way. The Holy Spirit can prompt you to do something but when you discuss it with others, your resolve may weaken. Although I would encourage you to listen to the advice of others, seek the Lord's answer in prayer. You will know if you are on the right track. Then be single-minded about your decision.

PRAYER
Heavenly Father
We come to this passage with caution. We want to praise and worship Jesus as the crowds did but we are also painfully aware that they would change their mind less than a week later. Help us to be wholly committed to Jesus and not to be double-minded. Holy Spirit we ask for your help with this. In the name of Jesus, we ask.
AMEN

BIBLE STUDY 6 – Questions

TESTING THE FACTS

1. What instructions did Jesus give to the two disciples at the Mount of Olives?

2. What happened when Jesus arrived in Jerusalem?

GIVING YOUR VIEW

1. Do places have atmosphere? Give examples of places you know. Share with the group.

2. Jesus' popularity in Jerusalem was based on his miracles (John 12: 18). He was soon out of favour. How authentic is being popular? Is it a value Christians should cultivate?

3. Examine the attitude of the Pharisees. There is always someone with a negative attitude. Do you agree? How would you deal with such a

person at an event in your church environment? Discuss in the group.

REFLECTION

James 1:6 But when he asks, he must believe and not doubt, because he who doubts is like a wave of the sea, blown and tossed by the wind. That man should not think he will receive anything from the Lord; he is a double-minded man, unstable in all he does.

BIBLE STUDY 7 - Monday's Bad Hair Day

FAITH

Read Mark 11: 12-26

After Jesus' celebratory entrance into Jerusalem, we are faced with the possibility that he may have got out of bed on the wrong side. In modern day terms we might describe it as a 'bad hair day'. What else could explain the cursing of the fig tree and the overturning of the tables in the temple? Why does Mark group the two incidents together?

Far from being an example of bad temper, I believe it demonstrates the heightened spiritual perception of Jesus. He was reaching his spiritual pinnacle. Both the showy leafy fig tree and the noisy traders displayed no signs of spiritual rejuvenation. The extravagance of fig leaves was at the expense of the fruit. Far from helping the worshippers, the traders are exploiting them. Jesus says (verse 17) that the temple must be a house of prayer. To other people a cursory glance at these two situations, betrayed no problem. But to Jesus, the lack of spiritual awareness was a disaster to the potential of the fig tree and the worshippers to salvation. He has come to save his people and evil forces are preventing that.

Continuing verses 20-26, Jesus expounds further on what has happened. Peter reminds Jesus what has happened to the fig tree as they pass it. The intention of the remark seems to be that Peter is amazed at the power of the curse Jesus issued. Jesus' reply concerns the faith that disciples must have. God hears the prayer of faith.

Echoing today's scripture are the words of James, "faith by itself, if it is not accompanied by action, is dead." (James 2:17)

PRAYER
Lord God, help us, through the power of the Holy Spirit, to have a spiritual awareness in everything we do. Give us the boldness to stand up for truth when the world blurs the distinction between the worldly and the spiritual.

We ask this in the name of Jesus.
AMEN.

BIBLE STUDY 7 – Questions

TESTING THE FACTS

1. What happened to the fig tree?

2. What was Jesus' attitude to the traders in the temple?

GIVING YOUR VIEW

1. Jesus' awareness of spiritual matters is superb. How can we be aware of the spiritual forces at work in the world? Discuss with the group.

2. What can we do when we are having a bad day? How can we help others when they seem to be having a bad day? Share with the group.

3. Do you get so caught up in everyday life that your spiritual awareness becomes blunted? Take a moment to ask the Lord to make you aware of the spiritual forces underlying events today both in the world and in your circle.

BIBLE STUDY 8 - Tuesday's Pot of Gold

WORSHIP

Read John 12: 1-11

How do you feel when a person makes a fuss of you? If someone says you can have a special treat, what would you choose? Would it be something to eat or drink or a visit to a special place? After a trying week behind him and a horrific death to come, Jesus appreciates the fuss that Mary makes of Him.

We are told that on Jesus' arrival in Bethany he goes to the house of Lazarus where a dinner is held in his honour. We are not told about any of the guests but we are told about Jesus' friend and his sisters. As expected, Martha is serving while Lazarus and Jesus are relaxing (v. 2). Then Mary does a strange thing. She takes a pint of pure nard and pours it on Jesus' feet. Usually, it would have been poured on someone's head. She has used so much that the whole house is filled with the perfume. This was Jesus' 'pot of gold' - the highlight of his most dreadful week on earth.

Jesus receives absolute adoration and affirmation from Mary, as the aroma of expensive perfume permeates the house. She wipes his feet with her hair. Was this a sort of foot massage? She does this risking the wrath of the whole company gathered there. It was considered inappropriate for a lady to let her hair be loose. She receives a commendation from Jesus. Jesus twinned this act with his burial. Already he is thinking of his death.

The other gospels record a similar event happening on Tuesday. Only Luke's version is placed earlier in Jesus' ministry. Time differences aside, I want to focus on how this event was pivotal to the recognition of Jesus. So many took him for granted as he ministered around the Galilean countryside. They came to expect healing, teaching and miracles. Most of the recipients didn't even come back to acknowledge him (the 9 lepers in Luke 17). Others gave up when they heard the level of commitment required. But Mary shows her appreciation of Jesus. She acknowledges his true worth. She worships Him. What about us? During this time of focussing on the pain and suffering Jesus endured, do we take time to worship Him?

Judas reveals his mean streak (verse 5) and demands that the money should have been used for the poor. He reprimands Mary. As I said before, there is always someone who will be negative. In a rare moment, Jesus defends a woman. He says, "Leave her alone."

PRAYER
Our Father,
Help us to appreciate Jesus. Help us to appreciate others. Show us through the power of your Holy Spirit, someone who we can do something special for.
In Jesus name.
AMEN

BIBLE STUDY 8 – Questions

TESTING THE FACTS

1.Describe what happened when Jesus visited Lazarus.

3. What did Jesus say about the perfume?

GIVING YOUR VIEW

1. Were you surprised at Jesus' attitude to Mary? What is your opinion about sharing with the poor? Do you consider that because you have earned your money, you should spend it on yourself? Share your ideas with the group.

2. Pray for an opportunity to show appreciation of someone you know. Be guided by the Holy Spirit in your choice. It may be someone not usually acknowledged for the Christian service they do.

3. What about the idea of the SECRET SANTA? Do we have to keep this for just Christmas time?
4. Does your church group take part in food banks or soup kitchens? Share your ideas.

PSALM 5:7

But I, by your great mercy will come into your house;

In reverence will I bow down toward your holy temple

BIBLE STUDY 9 - Beneath the Surface

BETRAYAL

Read: Luke 22: 3-6, 47, Matt 27: 1-10

Today we focus on the betrayer, Judas Iscariot, but we also keep in mind that Judas was being used by the powers of darkness. Although the bible says that Satan plays a part, Judas allows his mind and actions to be influenced. He was a responsible adult.

The act of betrayal is devastating. It is usually seen in our society in relationships. Cheating is commonplace. But there are other forms of betrayal which we might be guilty of. Disloyalty is present in divulging confidences, gossiping and lying. Disengagement in relationships whether friendships or love relationships is a form of emotional treason. By this I mean not caring enough to work on your relationship. Love demands attention. Jesus said this was the only way people could test our Christianity - that we love one another.

Sometimes betrayal in unintentional. I am reminded of a story my dad told us when we were children. He had been captured by the enemy in 1944 and with many others was ordered to march from Arnhem to Germany. No mean feat! When the soldiers reached the POW camp in Dresden, they were bombed by the Allies. My dad never forgot that and called it bad luck but I know he felt it was a betrayal by his country on brave soldiers. Several of his friends died in those raids.

Judas cold-heartedly discussed how he could betray Jesus. This was no spontaneous crime of passion. What was his motive? Thirty pieces of silver, estimated between R3000 and R9000 in today's money, is hardly a worthwhile sum. Judas' attitude of 'what's in it for me' often raises its head today. Guard against it.

Wednesday is a dark day for Jesus, even though it isn't apparent to others. Jesus knows Judas is putting his plans into operation to betray him.

Don't be overwhelmed by the 'dark nights of your soul' even if caused by yourself. Pray through them and fix your thoughts on Jesus (Hebrews 3: 1).

PRAYER

Almighty God,
As we realise Jesus was betrayed by someone who was supposed to be his friend, we ask you to help us when others let us down. Help us to work through the feelings of resentment, anger and revenge. Help us to forgive. Help us also to be reliable as friends to others.
We ask this in the name of Jesus.
AMEN.

BIBLE STUDY 9 – Questions

TESTING THE FACTS

1.Who did Judas go to? (See Matt 26:14, Luke 22:4)

2.What was the sign Judas gave so the chief priests could identify Jesus? (Luke 22:47)

GIVING YOUR VIEW

1. What forms can betrayal take in society? Discuss
   in the group different types of betrayal.

2. Betrayal has many victims in the fall-out. Think of who else was affected by Judas' actions. Share your ideas with the group.

3. What are some of the other forms of deceit which accompany betrayal? Share your ideas with the group.

Psalm 25:13
To you, O Lord, I lift up my soul;
In you I trust, O my God
Do not let me be put to shame, nor let my enemies
triumph over me.
No one whose hope is in your will ever be put to
shame.

BIBLE STUDY 10 - Thursday's Gethsemane Grief

PRAYER

Read: Mark 14: 32-42

So much happens on the Thursday that it is difficult to choose a focal point. Jesus washes the disciples' feet. He institutes the Lord's supper. He predicts Judas' betrayal and Peter's denial. He prays in the garden. He is arrested.

I am a keen gardener so I love the fact that Jesus sought solace in a garden. The prayer time in the garden of Gethsemane reveals Jesus is trapped in the frailty of a human body. It is a frailty which we share. Jesus and the disciples go to pray, as they would have done often. But as Jesus is praying a change comes over him. He becomes 'deeply distressed and troubled' (v. 33). The Holy Spirit is preparing him for a gruesome physical death. More than that, he will be separated from God. He will be in a void.

As realisation dawns, Jesus asks to be spared (v. 36). He does not demand. He asks in humility but admits the possibility that it may not be possible. Jesus perseveres and is able to find some acceptance of his situation.

The disciples could not help falling asleep. Jesus makes it clear that they were willing, but their bodies are weak (v. 38). As Jesus watches, he must have been aware that his physical body shared that vulnerability, and was sympathetic to the disciples. We are all limited by our physical bodies but we can develop our spiritual relationship with God so that we can rise above our human frailties. As Jesus proved at the time of the temptations.

PRAYER

Heavenly Father
We come in the name of Jesus; help us to take prayer more seriously. Prayer is your way of communicating with us. Help us to be willing to listen as well as talk. As we discover the intensity with which Jesus prayed, we are humbled. Help us Holy Spirit.
AMEN.

BIBLE STUDY 10 – Questions

TESTING THE FACTS

1. What did Jesus ask the disciples to do in the garden?

2. How successful were the disciples in this task?

GIVING YOUR VIEW

1. Think of a time when an answer to a prayer was not what you expected or wanted. How did you respond to God's answer? In hindsight, do you now understand why God answered as he did, or are you still struggling? If you are able, ask the group to pray with you.

2. Think about that evening before Jesus was arrested. Which part would you pick out as the most important? Share with the group.

PSALM 32:6

Therefore, let everyone who is godly pray to you while you may be found;

BIBLE STUDY 11 - The Dye is cast

FORGIVENESS

Read Luke 23: 32-43

On Good Friday it is traditional to reflect on what Jesus suffered: cross-examination, flogging, humiliation, degradation, physical torture, excruciating pain, brutality, abandonment, rejection. Jesus was innocent of the charges brought against him. Acknowledge the crucifixion on a personal level. Jesus suffered for you. Often churches hold services on this day which reflect in a quiet and sombre way.

The events of Good Friday are well documented in all four gospels. The stations of the cross traditionally record each detail of the suffering of Jesus. From his arrest through to questioning by Caiaphas and then being sent to Pilate there can only be one conclusion - crucifixion. It seems incredible that God would include this, in his plan of salvation for the world, the most horrific death imaginable for his son! But surely that is the point. Only the most gruesome death could fit the bill of atonement for the sins of the world.

The only reading appropriate for today must include the crux of salvation. Jesus says (v. 34),"Father forgive them for they do not know what they are doing."

Forgiveness lies at the heart of salvation. - not riches, power nor might. Our sin, the stain on the human heart, is forgiven through the death of Jesus. A message which is foolishness to those who are perishing becomes the power of God to those who are being saved. (1 Cor 1: 19). We have the choice whether we accept forgiveness from God through Jesus. If we do, we will start to look at the world through God's eyes.

PRAYER
Say the "Lord's prayer". Pay special attention to the words in verse 4,
"Forgive us our sins,
For we also forgive everyone who sins against us."

BIBLE STUDY 11 – Questions

TESTING THE FACTS

1. Consider each of the following phases of Jesus' suffering. Summarise each phrase with one word which conveys the emotion Jesus must have felt:

A) Peter's denial
B) the guards mock Jesus
C) Jesus stands before the Roman governor Pilate
D) Crowds shout "crucify him".
E) A notice is put above his cross "This is the King of the Jews"
F) Whipping and crucifixion
G) Darkness for three hours
H) Separation from God

GIVING YOUR VIEW

1. Spend some time meditating on your own. Write your own verse, poem or draw a picture to represent this special day, Good Friday.

Isaiah 53: 1-5

Who has believed our message and to whom has the arm of the Lord been revealed?

He grew up before him like a tender shoot, and like a root out of dry ground.

He had no beauty or majesty to attract us to him, nothing in his appearance that we should desire him.

He was despised and rejected by men, a man of sorrows, and familiar with suffering;

Like one from whom men hide their faces he was despised, and we esteemed him not.

Surely, he took up our infirmities and carried our sorrows,

Yet we considered him stricken by God, smitten by him, and afflicted.

But he was pierced for our transgressions, he was crushed for our iniquities;

The punishment that brought us peace was upon him, and by his wounds, we are healed.

BIBLE STUDY 12 - Calm before the storm

ANTICIPATION

Read Matthew 27: 57-66

Begin a cautious celebration because after the blackest ever Friday, Sunday is coming. I'm sure we have all had days which are so emotionally draining, that the next day we can do nothing but sit in despair. Maybe you are going through a dark time in your life. Be reassured it won't always be so bad. There is light in the darkness. That light is Jesus Christ.

Berg winds are well known in the Cape, South Africa. I lived there for eighteen years and it is something you never quite get used to. Unless you've experienced it, it is difficult to imagine. The air is warm yet calm. There is an eerie stillness but an awareness that the storm is coming. This is what Saturday was like. Jesus was dead. John records the soldier piercing Jesus' side to confirm death (John 19: 34). What is left to be done? For us the emotion is anticipation because we know the resurrection is coming but for the disciples, they probably experienced anxiety. They were unsure of their own future.

Joseph of Arimathea, one of the few rich disciples named in the gospels, seeks permission for the body to be buried. Pilate orders precautionary measures of sealing the tomb (v. 65). Just two women sit and wait opposite the tomb (v. 61). Were they the only two who had really listened to Jesus? Had they understood his message? Or were they there for another reason?

It seemed, as it so often does, that the forces of evil had won. But God had the last word. All the signs were there. The temple curtain had been torn in two. Holy people who had died were raised to life. Something special was about to happen. The earth was still. The heavens were about to explode in Resurrection power. But first came a time of waiting.

PRAYER

Almighty God, Lord Jesus and Holy Spirit,

We ask you to help us take in the amazing events of the Easter weekend. This day, after crucifixion and before resurrection was a time of despair and waiting.

It was a dreadful day indeed. Help us to use time like this to renew our strength. Help us to help others who may be in despair.

Amen.

.

BIBLE STUDY 12 – Questions

TESTING THE FACTS

1. What did Joseph of Arimathea do?

2. What were the names of the women sitting opposite the tomb?

GIVING YOUR VIEW

1. Think of a time when you have been waiting for something special to happen. It may have been the birth of a child, a wedding day, recovery from illness. Share with the group how you felt during this time. Was there anything you could do to ease the tension?

2. Do you doubt the resurrection of Jesus was a real event? Examine why you hold the views you do. Talk to other christians and read the scriptures analytically and prayerfully.

Isaiah 40: 29-31
He gives strength to the weary
And increases the power of the weak.
Even youths grow tired and weary
And young men stumble and fall;
But those who hope in the Lord
Will renew their strength.
They will soar on wings like eagles:
They will run and not grow weary,
They will walk and not be faint.

BIBLE STUDY 13 - Awesome Arising

CELEBRATION

Read Matthew 28: 1-10

We have something to celebrate! Whether it's watching an Easter parade or an Easter egg hunt on Table Mountain, find your own special way to celebrate today. One of my most unique memories is of waking up at St Antonio's guest house in Lindela, Mozambique to the sound of singing, drum beating and the sound of tambourines. It was so refreshing to experience another culture's celebration at Easter.

This week has been emotionally intense. Now comes the time to relax and rejoice. Make sure that you do. Do not let your busy life intrude on this day.

He has risen!
He has risen indeed!

PRAYER

Heavenly Father

What a day! Thank you for what you did in creating a plan for our salvation. Thank you, Lord Jesus, that you completed your mission. Thank you, Holy Spirit for the part you played. Help me to celebrate this great victory and to share with others when I have the opportunity.

AMEN

BIBLE STUDY 13 – Questions

GIVING YOUR VIEW

1. Which day of the week has been the most meaningful to you?

2. Imagine you had one week left on earth. How would you spend it? Think of Jesus' last week. Are there any points of comparison between your last week and His?

3. There have been many criticisms of the Resurrection story over the years. People have said:

   A) the women went to the wrong tomb.
   B) Jesus was not really dead and regained consciousness in the tomb. He then simply walked out.
   C) The body was taken by the authorities, by the disciples or by grave robbers.

Discuss in the group your answers to these

arguments. Are any of them convincing?

4. How do you celebrate Easter? Share with the
   group.

PSALM 145:7
They will tell of the power of your awesome
works, and I will proclaim your great deeds.
They will celebrate your abundant goodness and
joyfully sing of your righteousness;

BIBLE STUDY 14 – Upside down world

FOOTWASHING

Read John 13: 1-17

This bizarre incident provides another practical instruction from Jesus. Today, we have heard the story so often we accept it readily. But for the disciples this must have been akin to him pausing to put a child on his knee or talking to the marginalised, such as the Syrophoenician woman or the woman at the well. It just was not what they expected from their teacher.

John explains that it showed the extent of Jesus' love for them. It went beyond the boundaries of convention. This act, usual performed by a servant is performed by their master. It would be like the Queen coming to tea then doing the washing-up!

Washing, of course, was highly symbolic of the cleansing of the soul, as Peter learned. Jesus said,

"If you don't allow this, then you can have no part of me."

Jesus also refers to this feet-washing as a partial wash. They don't need a bath. They have already made a commitment to follow Jesus. They just need to be refreshed in their understanding.

Jesus also sets out the relationships between believers, as he says that they must now do this for each other. They must humble themselves before each other, by washing someone's feet, doing menial tasks. Also, they by logic, must be prepared for someone else to wash their feet. Maybe this is even more humbling.

BIBLE STUDY 14 – Questions

STATING THE FACTS

1. How does Peter respond to Jesus washing his feet? (v.8)
2. What does Jesus instruct the disciples to do (v.14)

GIVING YOUR VIEW

1. Have you ever attended a foot-washing service? Share with the group what your experience was.

2. What do you think Jesus was demonstrating?

3. Peter responds with horror at first. What is Peter's response after Jesus has explained?

4. How do you respond to church managerial structures in light of this passage. Share with the group.

BIBLE STUDY 15 - Fellowship Meal

COMMUNION

Read Matthew 26: 17-29, or Mark 14: 12-25,
Luke   22: 7-38, I Corinthians 11: 17-34

This passage is one with which most Christians
will be familiar, as the words are repeated every
Sunday in most churches and at least once a month
in others.

At first it seems odd that Jesus would give
thanks for the bread after they had started eating,
but then I remembered that the traditional Sabbath
meal is one where each of the foods is interspersed
with prayers. This meal after all was a Jewish
celebration.

In the traditional meal, the Jewish people
remember the passing of the angel of death over
the Hebrew houses in Egypt. It is already a
ceremony of remembrance. The difference is that
Jesus commands his disciples to remember him.

In Matthew's version, it is recorded that it is Judas who will betray Jesus. It is almost as if Jesus after the revelation about Judas, that is about betrayal, gives the disciples an act which will unify them and the Christians who come after them. Jesus drinks from the cup representing his blood. Judas will divide but Jesus will unify.

The synoptic gospel versions are each subtly different. Mark does not spell out that Judas is the traitor. Neither Matthew nor Mark record the words of remembrance. Luke records the cup is taken first and includes the words, "do this in remembrance of me". With the inclusion of the three versions of the same event, we get a complete and inclusive picture, as best as we can.

In the Corinthian record of the event in the early church, we must take Paul's aim in writing about it, to appreciate it. Paul is explaining that order and respect are important in the worship services. It seems the services did include communion. At the time Christians also had 'love feasts' (agape meals). Paul is distinguishing between the act of remembrance and disorderly conduct in eating when it forms part of the worship service. His letter is one of correction, so we don't get a complete picture of a communion service. In this Paul gives a warning about the seriousness of public commitment.

It is a reminder, as we come out of lockdown, that being a Christian is communal. We are part of a body and Jesus is the head of the body.

PRAYER

Lord Jesus
Help us to reflect on the meaning of communion.
Help us by the power of the Holy Spirit
To obey the command that Jesus has given us.
May we be mindful of the opportunity that it
presents to be of one mind with both Jesus and
fellow believers.
Thank you.

In the name of the Father, the Son
and the Holy Spirit.

AMEN

BIBLE STUDY 15 – Questions

STATING THE FACTS

1. What two food items are highlighted by Jesus at the meal with his disciples?

2. What is the name of the feast that Jesus and the disciples were celebrating?

GIVING YOUR VIEW

1.How does your group/church do "communion"? Share with the group and discuss the differences. Are the differences important?

2.In what ways is a communion service different from other services? Share your personal experience.

3.Luke's version (from verses 24-38) relates another incident which happened at the mealtime. Explain how Jesus uses this as a further picture of what it means to be a Christian.

FURTHER RESEARCH

Read Mark 14: 22-25 Think about the ways these verses are used by different churches today. Use the following information to start your discussion:

a) Mass - Catholic - the bread and wine actually become the body and blood of Jesus (transubstantiation).

b) Consubstantiation – Lutheran

c) Eucharist - Church of England

d) Communion/Lord's supper - Baptist, Methodist, other Free churches – the bread and wine are symbols representing the body and blood of Jesus.

Bibliography

NIV Study Bible, 1985, Zondervan Publishing House, General Editor, Kenneth Barke

Nouwen Henri J M,

The Return of the Prodigal   Son, 1994, Darton, Longman & Todd Ltd.
Gawande Atul, Being Mortal, 2015, Wellcome Collection
Editors Carson D A, France R T, Motyer J A, Wenham G J, New Bible Commentary, Protestant Book Centre, 1994.

L E N T

What can I give up for you?
I've been thinking it through and through.
I scratch my head, sieve my brain,
Wondering if it is insane.
Is there anything more I can do?
To help me draw closer to you?

Help me, Master, to hear your voice.
I feel that there is so much choice.
Will I give up treats or choc'lat?
Fast for days, pray blood in droplets?
No TV, games nor social media,
Could result in mild hysteria.

Lord Jesus, you have done it all.
Completed your mission 'midst pain and gall.
There is nothing left for me to achieve.
I must admit, it's quite a relief!
I can reflect on your perfect sacrifice,
Acknowledge you as the Holy Christ,
Bow the knee in complete submission.
There can be no repetition.

Crucifixion - John 15

"Is it finished? No, not yet."
It took hours, lest we forget.
"Oh Father," prayed Jesus on that night,
"I have done what you asked,
I have given them light.
I have healed the sick, the lame and the blind,
I have shown your love to all mankind.
And now I know it's over to you
To show them your final greatness too.
I have glorified you on this earth,
I've told them all about the new birth.
I pray for them and others thereafter
Give them hope, joy and laughter.
And now I am to be no more on this earth,
Keep them safe from all evil.
Sanctify them through your truth.
This is all I ask you Heavenly Father,
Keep them as one for ever after."

Then our Lord left that place.
He went into the garden.

He went for the human race.
"Is it finished … no not yet."
It went on for hours, lest we forget.

First came betrayal, let down by a friend,
As Judas lured him to His end.
The shock, the hurt, the pain was real.
There was no mitigation on this deal.
Smack went the fist of the soldier,
Who demanded an answer now.
"The High Priest is talking to you.
You must bend the knee and bow."
Pain of the bonds that bound Him
As they dragged Him before Pilate,
Echoed the hurt of denial
As Peter stood before the firelight.
Back then to Herod who clothed Him
In stripes of purple and red,
Covered His back in agony
As the wounds wept through and bled.
He knew it had to happen
But it didn't deaden the pain,
As they shouted, "Crucify Him,
We want Barabbas again."
Pilate then took his whip
And beat Him again, nearly dead.
There was no one to comfort Him.

The disciples, they had all fled.
They platted a crown of thorns
And crammed it upon His brow,
That sweated blood and teardrops.
What else could they do to Him now?

Clink, clink went the sound of the hammer,
Which nailed Him to the tree.
Sighs and sobs of His mother
as He endured this blasphemy.
As His agony now unfolded
He realised its terrible price:
Separation from God, unbearable;
Total blackness must suffice.
"It is finished," cut His voice through the silence.
A knife through His Father's heart.
"It is finished," came the echo through the ages.
Jesus had played His part.

Holy Communion

I remember you died for me Lord
As I take this bread today.
I remember all your agony;
You're the Truth, the Life, the Way.
I come to you, pride all gone
To free me from my sins.
I remember the peace you gave
The day I asked you in.

Forgive me for my anger
When self has come to the fore,
When the devil has been prowling around
Howling at my door.
I've told him I belong to You.
He must run away.
I've told him I'm trusting You
Until the Judgement Day.

I remember You, Lord.
As I take this cup today.
You served others with humility,
Didn't care what Pharisees would say.
Keep me ever conscious of all the lost souls.
Help me to reach out to them
And bring them in your fold.
Give me all compassion to heal those who are ill.
Give me the satisfaction of doing God's will.

I remember You, Lord
And know t'was a sinner like me
Who betrayed You in the garden -
Grant me humility.

So, Lord as I remember You
I give you all the praise and worship due.
I'll know you'll remember me, Lord.
When I get to Heaven;
When the sheep and the goats are sorted
When the final judgement is given.

Celebration

Come celebrate, bring your praise!
The king of glory has numbered days.
Crowds surround Him. They're filled with joy
for the Healer, Prophet, Joseph's boy.
It's been a long and dusty road.
Disciples, unaware, an ill wind bodes.
Miracles on the way abounded.
The intellectual mind confounded.
Blind Bartimaeus received his sight,
calling 'Son of David' with all his might.
Pilgrims, children, all are blessed
by Zaccheus' self-invited guest.
He was moved to help the poor,
When Jesus exploded through his door.
Two disciples sent to find the donkey
to transport the man born of Mary.
They threw their cloaks upon its back,
Faces set to Jerusalem, trudging down the track.
People waving hosanna branches,
express celebration dances.
In sweet abandonment dismiss all doubt.
If they don't the very stones will cry out.
They've seen the dead, to life raised.
How can they not give God all praise?

Model Answers

Bible Study 1 **REPENTANCE**
The Facts:

1.Verse 9 says, "You struck down Uriah the Hittite with the sword and took his wife to be your own." 2 Samuel 11:14 further says, "in the morning David wrote a letter to Joab and sent it with Uriah. 'Put Uriah in the front line where the fighting is fiercest. Then withdraw from him so he will be struck down and die.'" So, David was guilty of the murder of Uriah and adultery with his wife Bathsheba.

2.Verse 14 tells us that God told David that his son will die.

Giving your view:
1.I have attended an Ash Wednesday service through the Church of England but as I now

worship with a free church, they usually don't have Ash Wednesday services.

2.I understand that repentance means turning away from the wrong things I do and turning towards God.

3.I think David's punishment seems harsh. It seems unfair to the innocent child but as the king, David had extra responsibility to set an example to the people.

Bible Study 2 **FASTING**

The Facts:

1.These comments were made by Jesus when he taught the disciples on the mountain. Usually this is referred to as the 'Sermon on the Mount'.
2.Jesus instructs the disciples not to look 'glum'. Dress as you would every day so it is not obvious to others that you are fasting.

Giving Your View:
1.My idea of fasting is to go without food for a period of time which you decide before you start. I don't think the denial of pleasure or enjoyment is

the same as going without food. Food is an essential, pleasure isn't.

2.I believe when it helps and encourages others it is good to disclose you are fasting. It must never be disclosed as a boast or to compete with other Christians.

3.Yes, I believe that all Christian leaders should fast regularly except if there are medical conditions which prohibit it. Spiritual fasting helps us to have control over some of our bodily urges and instincts.

4.Jesus will not be inhibited by the 'rules. His illustration emphasises that he wanted his disciples to enjoy his company while he was on earth. Today, I think we must not allow ourselves to be regulated by rules but follow the lead of the Holy Spirit. Sometimes fasting is appropriate and sometimes it is not but we can only know through prayer and the guidance of the Holy Spirit.

Bible Study 3 **TEMPTATION**
The Facts:

1.The three temptations were a) to satisfy his hunger b) to take God's protection for granted 3) to desire earthly power, wealth and success.

2.The scripture verses were:

Matthew 4:4 "It is written, Man does not live on bread alone, but on every word that comes from the mouth of God."

Matthew 4:7 "It is also written: Do not put the Lord your God to the test."

Matthew 4:10 Jesus said to him, "Away from me, Satan. For it is written, Worship the Lord your God and serve him only."

Giving Your Views:

1.I have several weaknesses. I know I find it difficult to control my eating, especially in not eating too many cakes and biscuits. I find relationships with the opposite sex difficult. So, my weaknesses lie in the first temptation.

2.Modern day examples of weaknesses are the temptation to eat too much or too little, having relationships outside of marriage. Sometimes Christians put themselves in danger claiming that God will protect them. Thirdly many people are obsessed in the modern world with technology and television.

3.I do memorise scripture verses. I find it useful in times of trouble and weakness.

4.One example is that some Christians are not being vaccinated against the covid-19 virus claiming God will protect them.

5.Worship means giving all your attention, your time and putting something first in your life. We know this place should be reserved for God.

Bible Study 4 **EVIL**

The Facts:

1.Luke's report implies that it is a demon which is causing dumbness.

2.Jesus says a kingdom divided in itself will fall. If Jesus was working for the devil, he would not have done the good of healing the man.

3.Jesus has just been teaching about prayer.

Giving Your Views:

1.I do believe there is a presence of evil in the world. We may not be able to see evil spirits but we can feel a malevolence. There is no doubt that people can do evil things.

2.Yes, we can sometimes see the same type of illness in modern days but we don't put the same psychological names to them. This is a very complex area.

3.Yes, we must be very careful to understand whether someone is suffering from a mental health issue or if there is a presence of evil. We can only probably know the difference through prayer and the Holy Spirit's discernment.

Bible Study 5 **SACRIFICE**
The Facts:

1.John the Baptist lived in the desert. His clothes were very basic. His food was simple – wild locusts and honey.

2.John's disciples asked Jesus in Matthew 11: 2 "Are you the one who was to come or should we expect someone else?

3.In Matthew 14: 8 it reports that Salome asked for the head of John the Baptist on a platter.

Giving your views:

1.I would tell John of the miracles Jesus did to heal people, and of the profundity of his teachings.

2.I appreciate the ministry of John the Baptist. I find it easy to follow the rules and feel safe when I know how I should behave. However, I know it is probably 'better' to be more like Jesus, that is a risk-taker and spontaneous.

3.I would have been scared to say anything to a man in such a wealthy and powerful position.

4.I think many people act out of ignorance and the poor teaching they receive. They are influenced by other people. A lot of people find it difficult to control their own instincts.

5.The values of God are miles away from the values of society. Society values success, and money. These are not on God's agenda. There is a lack of purity in society. Most people do not even know what sort of lifestyle God wants from us.

Bible Study 6 **DOUBLE-MINDEDNESS**
The Facts:

1.Jesus said to the two disciples, "Go to the village where you will find a colt. Untie it and bring it here. If you are challenged say that the Lord has need of it."

2.When Jesus arrived in Jerusalem he cried because the people of the city did not appreciate who he was, and the opportunity would be lost.

Giving your views:

1.Yes, I do believe that places have an atmosphere. I also think that where you are in the world matters. For example, in warm climates people seem to be more relaxed than in cold countries.

2.I think everyone has a desire to be popular. It is difficult to say what makes a person popular. Often it has to do with how a person looks. This is sad. We must remember that God looks at the heart. In this context, I think of when Israel wanted a king they chose a tall good-looking guy, Saul but God chose a shepherd boy.

3.Yes, there is always someone ready to point out what you are doing wrong instead of focussing on what you are doing well. I try to ignore negative attitudes and remarks and say something positive instead.

Bible Study 7 **FAITH**

The Facts:

1.Jesus cursed the fig tree and it withered and died.

2.Jesus overturned the tables of the money changers and the benches of those selling doves. He would not let anyone carry goods through the temple courts.

Giving Your Views:

1.If we want to be aware of spiritual matters we need to slow down! We should sit quietly and reflect on the world today and maybe read from the bible and pray. We certainly need to shut out the busy world for a while.

2.When things are going wrong, we should sit down and take a break from our busy lives. Maybe sit in a garden for a while. Going for a walk also helps us to relax. We should try to encourage others to do this. Being calm ourselves can help others to be calm.

There are certainly times when I become engulfed with the busyness of the day.

Bible Study 8 **WORSHIP**
The Facts:

1.When Jesus visited Lazarus, Martha was as usual serving the dinner. Mary by contrast suddenly takes out pure nard, a very expensive oil, and pours it over Jesus' feet. Then she wipes his feet with her hair.

2.Jesus was pleased that Mary had showed such devotion. He soaks up the atmosphere and tells the others not to be cross with her.

Giving Your Views:

1.I think there is a time and place for everything. I was surprised that Jesus was pleased but considering Mary was prompted by the Holy Spirit then the mystery disappears.

2.Poverty is a relative concept. That means that what we might consider poverty another country might think was luxury.

3.I walk around my village and pray for the people I meet.

4.We participated in a Secret Santa in our homegroup. I was surprised that some people didn't want to take part. What a great idea to do it at other times of the year.

Bible Study 9 **BETRAYAL**
The Facts:
  1.Judas went to the chief priests.
  2.The sign Judas gave was a kiss.

Giving Your Views:

1.Betrayal is not a word which is used in society today. Betrayal in relationships is often not recognised and is taken casually. Gossiping is a common pastime today and people don't see anything wrong with it.

2.Judas' actions would have affected all the other disciples. It would also have affected the family of Jesus, his mother and his brothers and sisters and cousins.

3.Telling lies and taking part in secrecy would be part of the deceit.

Bible Study 10 **PRAYER**
The Facts:
1.Jesus asked the disciples to sit down while he prayed.
2.The disciples were not able to stay awake. They fell asleep.

Giving Your Views:
1.There have been so many times when the answer to prayer is not what I wanted or expected. I acknowledge that God is sovereign and he can answer prayers how he likes.
2.I think the most important event on this evening was the prayer time with Jesus. It was so important because I know how unsuccessful most of us are at praying and being found faithful in prayer.

Bible Study 11 **FORGIVENESS**
The Facts:
 1 A) sadness
   B) pity
   C) superiority
   D) surprise
   E) satisfaction

F) pain
G) wonder
H) despair

Giving Your Views:
1.See my poem "Crucifixion"

Bible Study 12 **ANTICIPATION**
The Facts:
1.He went to Pilate and asked for the body of Jesus.
2.Mary Magdalene and Mary wife of Clopas.

Giving Your Views:
1.Yes, when I was pregnant for the first time and waiting for the birth, I felt anxious and unsure because I did not know what to expect. I was looking forward to seeing the baby. I read a lot so I used to do that to relax.
2.I absolutely believe in the resurrection. I believe Almighty God can do anything within the boundaries of his own character and morality.

Bible Study 13 **CELEBRATION**
Giving Your Views:
1.Sunday, the day of resurrection is the most special for me.

2.I believe we must be in a continual state of readiness that it could indeed be our last week. I'd try to finish one of my writing projects. I'd make sure everything financial was tied up so as not to leave any problems for my children. Other than that, I wouldn't do anything differently from what I do today.

3.I do not think any of these are strong arguments.

4.At Easter I love to go to church to celebrate. I buy my grandchildren Easter eggs. I like to have a good celebration meal, usually turkey.

Bible Study 15 **FOOTWASHING**

The Facts:

1.Peter said to Jesus, "no, you will never wash my feet."

2.Jesus commands the disciples to wash one another's feet. This is also symbolic to represent that Christians should not 'lord' it over one another.

Giving Your View:

1.Yes, I have attended a foot-washing service. Only three people of the congregation were asked if they would allow someone to wash their feet. I wasn't one of them. I was glad at the time that I wasn't asked. The people found this act a humbling experience.

2.Jesus was demonstrating that a leader must be the servant of the people. Jesus as the master completed a menial task for his disciples.

3.Peter's response is over the top again. I suppose that was part of his personality. His response is to ask Jesus then to wash the whole of him.

4.I am horrified by the structures of many churches, especially where there is a hierarchy of bishops and elders. The ordained minister is there, separated and trained to teach the bible and lead the congregation in prayer and by example. All the believers should be actively participating in the activities of the church.

Bible Study 15 **COMMUNION**

The Facts:

1.The two food items were bread and wine.

2.There are several small differences in the accounts. Mark does not say the traitor is Judas. Matthew and Mark do not mention the words about remembrance. Luke mentions the cup first before the bread. The Corinthian passage adds a strong warning to examine yourself. That is an interesting difference.

3.This version recalls an incident when the disciples are arguing over who is the greatest. This is ironical isn't it, as Jesus has just demonstrated that a hierarchy of greatest and least is not appropriate for Christians

Notes for Group Leaders

1.These studies are intended not only for individual study but for groups. This means that groups may not have time to work through all the questions. It is up to the group leader to choose which questions she/he thinks is the most appropriate for their group.

2.It is the responsibility of the group leader to set aside adequate preparation for the study. This will include prayer for themselves and each member of the group. Ideally the group should be about 8 members. It could be extended to 12 but bear in mind that does cut down the time for each person to respond. For each member to grow in their Christian life, it is necessary for them to participate. This, however, may take a few weeks and if someone really does not want to speak, their wishes should be respected.

3.Encourage openness. Remind everyone that any personal details revealed during a group session is not a titbit to gossip about but must remain in the group. There may be occasions when a participant should be encouraged to have an individual prayer session so that the bible study can be continued. Decisions of this nature should be taken by the group leader.

4. Your role as leader of the group is to ensure every member has the opportunity to respond, should they want to. Make sure no one or two people dominant the group. A kind reminder to listen to others may be necessary.

5. Where possible set the time boundaries so that participants know the group will start on time and finish on time. Start the group time with a simple prayer, which can be written down beforehand if you are not used to spontaneous prayer.

6. Encourage each member to buy their own bible study book so they can write their own personal notes in the book. This commitment will encourage a development of faith and will enable participants to re-use the studies at a later date. Encourage each member to bring their own bible.

7. Remember that each participant will be at a different stage of Christian maturity. Each contribution made to the group should be encouraged, however simple. Remind the group that this is a group exercise, and members will be building each other up.

About The Author

Born in London, Rosalie Weller trained as a teacher as a mature student. She moved to South Africa in 1981 with her husband Syd who was pursuing a naval career. Touched by the poverty of the community, she taught English in a township, as well as bringing up their five children as a military wife.

Rosalie managed a church soup kitchen in the same township, which gradually developed into a cross-cultural project as apartheid began to disintegrate. It soon included multi-racial church services, children's groups and a clothing distribution self-help scheme.

After studying at the Bible Institute of South Africa in Kalk Bay and the University of Cape Town, she was ordained in the Uniting Presbyterian Church of Southern Africa. She accepted a post as Assistant Minister at Fish Hoek Presbyterian Church until in 2001 she was called to a missionary post in Gloucestershire, England.

Rosalie has travelled extensively in Africa, including Botswana, Zambia, Namibia, Zimbabwe and Mozambique, taking the opportunity to teach and preach as the occasion arose.

In 2004, at the end of the contract with the Council for World Mission, Rosalie developed the Religious Studies and PSHE departments as the Head of Ethics Faculty in a state school in England.

She is currently living in England and is involved  in a renovation project with her husband, besides writing bible studies, historical fiction and poetry. She runs a successful Writing Circle and has a YouTube channel. (Reverend Rosalie Weller)

Afterword

If you have enjoyed this bible study, why not let me know. I can be contacted at email: rosalieweller70@gmail.com, www.rosalieweller.com, Instagram rosalie_weller, Facebook Reverend Rosalie Weller@ trustintheLordJesus and on YouTube – Reverend Rosalie Weller

Other Books in this series

The Book of Hebrews

This collection of 10 Bible Studies is for mature Christians. It tackles the thorny issue of giving up on your faith. At the end of each chapter there are thought-provoking questions to challenge the group. At the end of the book, there are model answers for individuals to compare their own study answers. Two original poems by the author are included.

The Prison Letters

This collection of 12 Bible Studies is on the letters Paul wrote to the churches while he was in prison in Rome. (Philemon, Ephesians, Colossians and Philippians) Each study is followed by questions which can be used as part of a group bible study. At the end of the book there are model answers which will be particularly valuable for anyone studying as an individual.

Tell Me the Stories of Jesus

This collection of 12 bible studies is based on the gospel of Luke. Each study features a unique part of Jesus' life. At the end of each study there are thought-provoking questions for use at group bible studies. At the end of the book there are model answers to help any individuals studying on their own.

David - Man for our Times

This is a collection of 10 Bible Studies based on the life of King David. Called a man after God's own heart, David was not perfect. These studies engage the reader to explore David's life. At the end of each chapter there are questions suitable for use in groups. Model answers at the back of the book can be used for individual study.

Is Faith enough? – A study of the book of James

These 12 studies explore the controversial book of James. The studies include a comparison between Paul's assertion that faith is the most important factor and James' idea that faith must be accompanied by deeds.

Pandemic Peaces

This journal will encourage those struggling through bereavement and loss. Besides an honest account through her own pain, Rosalie includes original poems and images to be reflected on. Each chapter begins with a scripture verse which serves as the devotional focus.

Printed in Great Britain
by Amazon

77212727R00085